RETURNING TO THE CIVIL WAR

GRAND REENACTMENTS OF AN ANGUISHED TIME

Photographs by
AL THELIN

Written by
KENT COURTNEY

GIBBS·SMITH
PUBLISHER

SALT LAKE CITY

To my wife and children
 for putting up with a
 wandering soul;
to Borge Andersen
 for bringing light and shadow
 into my world;
to my mother
 for cultivating my right brain;
to the spirit of the men and women
 who lost their lives in a cause
 they believed in.
  A.T.

To April and Julie Courtney,
 whose sacrifices made this
 book possible.
  K.C.

99 98 97 3 2 1
Text copyright © 1997 by Kent Courtney
Photographs © 1997 by Al Thelin

This is a Peregrine Smith Book, published by
Gibbs Smith, Publisher
P.O. Box 667
Layton, Utah 84041

Design by J. Scott Knudsen, Park City, Utah
Printed and bound in Hong Kong

Library of Congress Cataloging-in-Publication Data

Courtney, Kent.
    Returning to the Civil War : grand reenactments of an
    anguished time / written by Kent Courtney : pho-
    tographed by Al Thelin. —1st ed.
        p. cm.
      "This is a Peregrine Smith book"—T.p. verso.
    ISBN 0-87905-783-1
        1. United States—History—Civil War, 1861–1865.
    2. Historical reenactments—United States.   I. Thelin, Al.
    II. Title.
    E468.9.C68   1997
    973.7—dc20   96-41231
                        CIP

CONTENTS

Literally thousands of people have led me toward being a historian, an interpreter of America's musical heritage and the author of this book. I wish to thank them all.

Hundreds of event coordinators and sponsoring organizations have opened the door to my participation at reenactments. Civil War Round Tables and historical societies have nurtured my understanding as a student and as a lecturer. Veterans organizations, particularly many camps of the Sons of Confederate Veterans, have aided me with moral and financial support.

To my fellow reenactors and to the spectators whose enthusiasm keeps me motivated in my pursuits, I owe a large debt of thankfulness.

Thank you to Cathy Clarke of Historical Treasures, whose logistical support made this book possible. I also thank Madge Baird and Gibbs Smith for encouraging this project.

I particularly thank those who have set aside historic sites and saved them as parks and museums. Because of their foresight and dedication, my parents were able to take me to battlefields, giving me an early awareness of the importance of preserving history.

KENT COURTNEY

As I have traveled the country going from battle to battle, many wonderful people sacrificed their time so I could get the great photos. To all of them I am grateful. I marched into battle beside many troops and shared in their victories and defeats—to these men and ladies, thank you for the privilege. Many fine people shared fires and wedge tents with me and offered me rides. Thank you to all those strangers who offered me kind words and compassion in those lonely moments on the road. Thanks to my editor, Madge Baird, and to my publisher, Gibbs Smith, for their faith.

Thanks to the many companies who helped in my quest: Borge B. Andersen & Associates; Inkleys; Fuji Film, Inc.; Royce Photographic; Wasatch Photo; Picture Line; Patrick McHugh; Andrew, Jackie & Ron King; Fort McHenry National Monument and Historic Shrine; Fort Ward Museum & Historic Site, City of Alexandria, VA; Navy Museum, Washington Naval Yard; Victoria and the Southern Rifle Guard; Richard Phren.

AL THELIN

Becoming a Time Traveler

O n the sacred ground of honor, men shout themselves hoarse, burn their fingers on hot rifles, and blacken themselves with the soot of gunpowder as they march shoulder to shoulder in determined array. True fear sets in as the enemy comes closer. Could the spirits of fallen soldiers be circulating among this crowd of Civil War reenactors? To the onlooker it may seem like mass hypnosis, but to the reenactor it's real—as overwhelming as any religious experience.

Thunderous roars of rifle volleys are fired and comrades fall in the mock throes of death. The sorrow felt for them is genuine as the battle line tramps forward and generals move the soldiers around as pawns in the same way that soldiers were moved in the 1860s. Although the outcome is sure, the battle strategies are known only to a select few.

Northern troops hold off an advance of determined Southerners on sacred ground of honor.

CREATING A SPIRITUAL EXPERIENCE

More than make-believe, Civil War reenacting is total immersion into the time period of the War. It is the feeling, the guts, the fears, the spirit of actually being in the 1860s.

In some ways, a reenactment is a large-scale seance held in broad daylight with dozens or thousands of other people. The spiritual experience comes like a flash in a time warp wherein the window has opened up and the reenactor has seen a former life. Days long gone grow alive inside the person. In the middle of the battle, the goose bumps hit, a coldness runs up and down the spine. There is a spiritual awakening that tingles in the brain; then suddenly, he's there.

A person can travel back in time on the dance floor. As dancers twirl in a Virginia reel, ball gowns flow over the floor like slowly spinning tops. Shouts accompany a couple's sashay down the dance aisle as everyone claps to the beat. In the candlelight the women are beautiful and the men are dashing. Somewhere in the cavorting, time slips back to the elegance and honor of a culture gone with time. For the night, the reenactors belong to the upper crust of society.

A medical staff cares for wounded. One man screams in mock pain as a minié ball is removed from a raw chicken breast that has been taped to his arm. Through the blood-stained shirt, the poultry flesh simulates the arm that would have been treated with primitive surgical instruments of the war. Nurses wipe fake blood from the wound that oozes from a small plastic hose that pumps the liquid from a bottle under the table. To the spectator, a reenactment is almost like watching a stage play, but to the reenactor it all feels real.

An officer of a Confederate reenactment unit addresses a crowd at an old cemetery. "For those who have gone before us, we gather here. We represent those Georgia men who gave either part of their lives or their whole lives for the cause."

In front of several grave markers, reenactors stand at attention. One of the soldiers, a

private, steps forward, holding a lighted candle lantern. "I am Private James Wellburn. I was born in Clinton, Georgia, in 1841. I enlisted in the Georgia Militia and served with the Confederate Army. I fought many battles but lost my life defending Atlanta. My brother found my body and brought it back to Clinton. Here I lie in service to God." Shivers overtake the onlookers as the candle is blown out, and those attending this ceremony are brought into a oneness of spirit.

In another place, another time, a lady tucks her hair into a soldier's hat, dirties her face and dons a loose-fitting uniform that hides her figure. She practices the facial expressions of a warrior, trying to look mean and masculine. This gender-jumping allows her to experience

The blood and drama become too real in this field hospital.

Hundreds of wedge tents in close proximity re-create a real Civil War atmosphere.

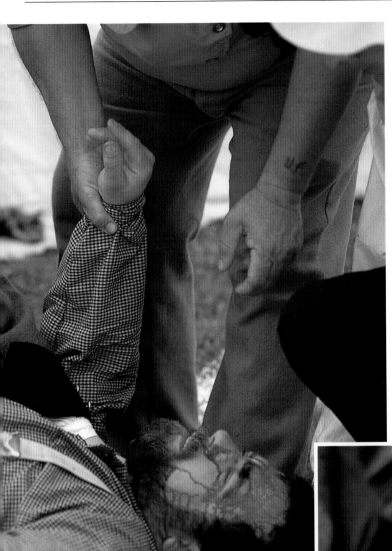

Above: Standing by the grave, this reenactor pays tribute to fallen Confederate soldiers.

After battle, sitting among the men, a woman soldier sips water to cool down from the intense heat.

Women help the men by joining a Soldiers Aid Society and making socks and such.

the feelings her ancestors had on the battlefield. It is an act, and she gets ready for her part. "She" becomes "he" in a new existence.

At a campfire, legends about the daring exploits of patriots are passed around. The American Iliad is recounted as an oral tradition. The telling becomes a part of the episode as well as a creation of the experience. Bravery is praised. Foolishness brings laughter.

"Where?"

"Down on South Street drinking gin."

"Right." And the words of a popular drinking song are sung in the Union Army camp by soldiers well versed in having a good time. By the moon and candlelight, guitars, accor-

dions, mandolins, banjos and harmonicas join the voices of soldiers lost in the good times of the war. A bones player rattles accompaniment with a tambourine man while another taps a spoon on the bottom of a tin cup.

In another scene, a distinguished senator in civilian attire speaks to soldiers from his home state of Illinois. "I am visiting your camp to show the personal interest I have in your well-being and to demonstrate the support I have in your effort to ensure a victory for our glorious cause," the senator says as he shakes hands with his constituents. "I would be most pleased if you would remember me when your opportunity to vote comes."

In another part of Federal camp, "Colonel, we need clean sinks; this vile smell is bringing disease and contagion to our men. If the filth doesn't kill them, it will impair their ability to fight," a lady from the Sanitary Commission pleads in an unscripted scene.

The reenacting colonel plays along and improvises his response. "Madam, I am very pleased to know your concerns for our men and you are right. Moreover, we march today, leaving this reminder to the secessionists of what multiple penalties will be brought to them for their treasonous actions. Let us leave these dirty sinks in their land so that they may remember the stench of their rebellion."

Over in the Confederate camp, a lady explains in a southern drawl, "I do everything I can for the cause. I joined the Soldiers Aid Society because they know where help is needed. They told me the men march so much that they wear out socks faster than most anything. If making socks helps them march quickly, then the war will be over sooner."

"I've got biscuits and gravy. Come get some. I'm not gonna tell y'all where I got this meat, but it's good and not too salty. I wish I could have fed Joe before he was killed at Pittsburgh Landing," she explains as she spoons the steamy mixture onto a soldier's tin plate. "Eat up and stay strong so you can get back at the Yanks." The wood smoke from her fire blends with the aroma of the sage seasoning, and everyone is hungry. She feeds soldiers

GOOBER PEAS

Sitting by the roadside on a summer day,
Chatting with my messmates, passing time away,
Lying in the shadow underneath the trees,
Goodness, how delicious, Eating Goober Peas!
CHORUS (repeat after each verse):
Peas! Peas! Peas! Peas! Eating Goober Peas!
Goodness, how delicious, eating Goober Peas!

When a horseman passes, the soldiers have a rule,
To cry out at their loudest, "Mister, here's your mule."
But another pleasure enchantinger than these,
Is wearing out your grinders, eating Goober Peas!

Just before the battle, the Gen'ral hears a row.
He says, "The Yanks are coming, I hear their rifles now."
He turns around in wonder, and what do you think he sees?
The Georgia Militia eating Goober Peas!

I think my song has lasted almost long enough,
The subject's interesting, but rhymes are mighty rough,
I wish the war was over when free from rags and fleas,
We'd kiss our wives and sweethearts and gobble Goober Peas!

"**F**ourscore and seven years ago our fathers brought forth on this continent, a new nation, conceived in Liberty, and dedicated to the proposition that all men are created equal.

"Now we are engaged in a great civil war, testing whether that nation or any nation so conceived and so dedicated, can long endure. We are met on a great battle-field of that war. We have come to dedicate a portion of that field as a final resting place for those who here gave their lives that that nation might live. It is altogether fitting and proper that we should do this.

"But, in a larger sense, we cannot dedicate—we cannot consecrate—we cannot hallow—this ground. The brave men, living and dead, who struggled here, have consecrated it, far above our poor power to add or detract. The world will little note, nor long remember what we say here, but it can never forget what they did here. It is for us the living, rather, to be dedicated here to the unfinished work which they who fought here have thus far so nobly advanced. It is rather for us to be here dedicated to the great task remaining before us—that from these honored dead we take increased devotion to that cause for which they gave the last full measure of devotion—that we here highly resolve that these dead shall not have died in vain— that this nation, under God, shall have a new birth of freedom—and that government of the people, by the people, for the people, shall not perish from the earth."

ABRAHAM LINCOLN
GETTYSBURG ADDRESS

until the black iron pot is empty, dedicating her life for the cause that cost her husband's life.

In the 1860s the United States was divided in sharp argument over a number of political and economic questions. The ultimate question was "Does a state have the right to remove itself from the Union?" Throughout the loyal portion of the United States as well as those areas in rebellion known as the Confederacy, people mustered into militia groups and joined the armies to fight for what they believed. At home and in the fields of war, men, women and children did what they could to support the cause that they felt was right.

For many, the main draw of Civil War reenacting is the opportunity to "teach and show history from a more personal level," according to Blaine Piper, who has been involved in

Styles of clothing vary widely, but period correctness is the pride of every reenactor.

these reenactments for eighteen years. They love to wear the clothes, present a true picture of the causes that resulted in a bloody strife, and show how it affected the people of that period.

The word *period* takes on a whole new meaning in the context of reenacting. It refers to the recreation of all the outside attire associated with the 1860s as well as the inside attitudes and feelings of the individuals and groups living at this time. *Period correct* means that some thing or action or manner of speaking would have been correct in the 1860s. Taken to its farthest limits, period-correct behavior becomes a first-person impression: an individual recreates the persona of an 1860s resident and is, from time to time, privileged to experience that uncanny feeling of being a time traveler.

Over years of participation, reenactors fill their memories with their favorite experiences. For J. C. Nobles, it was "memorial services answering the roll of honor at Old Clinton Methodist Church cemetery." Blaine Piper recalls "getting up early in the morning from a camp in Kentucky, marching over the Cumberland Gap, through Virginia, into Tennessee for an afternoon battle." One of those moments for Stephen B. McKinney, a seventeen-year reenactor, was "the 130th Murfreesboro lying as a casualty in front of a burning house and watching the Texas Brigade make an assault."

Another reenactor, Martin C. J. Mongiello, cherishes the time he was "aboard the replica C.S.S. *Virginia* ironclad, fighting the U.S.S. *Monitor,* and had the U.S. Postal Service first-day stamp revealed with our battle on it."

"Our most memorable event," recount Mark and Meg DeAngelis, "occurred at Colt State Park in Bristol, Rhode Island. We had the unique experience of having our younger daughter christened at this event. We conducted the ceremony in the outdoor chapel with the crash and rattle of musketry and guns resounding about us. Our entire regiment was held out of battle until the ceremony was completed, then the regiment pulled out from the ceremony and formed ranks. Both the period

and modern civilians remaining sang out the familiar refrain 'Amazing Grace.' In the background, soldiers counted out in ranks while scabbards and tin cups clanked as they marched off to war. It was one of the moments that we refer to as 'wrinkles in time.'"

Many interesting specialties are re-created, such as those who communicated on the battlefield in the Signal Corps. Founded during the Civil War, the Signal Corps had an influence on the outcome of battles and is a high-profile part of large reenactments.

A cluster of period-correct rifles at rest adds to the authenticity of the camp.

REENACTMENT VARIETIES

Many types of events are Civil War reenactments. Some are held annually, some come around every two to five years, and some happen only once and never again. A huge event such as the one at Murfreesboro, Tennessee, may draw thousands of participants and even more spectators, while some living-history events are small, with a few soldiers and civilians demonstrating life during the war.

Battle reenactments are often held on or near the ground where the real battle took place. Many think of this as the purest form of reenactment and claim that contact with the spirits of soldiers who died in the battlefield is a possibility. But some battle re-creations are held far from the original battlefield. An example is the staging in Newark, Ohio, of the battle of Kennesaw Mountain, which took place in Georgia. Spectators and reenactors benefit by re-creating a historical event without having to travel to the original site.

A **tactical** is a judged skirmish where the outcome is determined by points earned. This is usually for reenactors only and typically includes running battles through the woods. Scenarios are set up to test a unit's response to particular situations. It is sort of like paintball fighting without the paint.

A **plantation reenactment** takes place at a historic site that is already set up to draw tourists. Usually there is a lot of drilling and several small-scale skirmishes to demonstrate fighting tactics. Oak Alley in Louisiana is an example of this type of event and even features

A tactical in the woods at Resaca, Georgia.

Women enjoy one another's company at a plantation home in Tunnel Hill, Georgia.

live firing of cannons in target competition.

Fort reenactments occur across the country. The forts are permanent installations that have been preserved, rebuilt or reconstructed. The lodgings can be very pleasant, and there is a unique atmosphere at a fort. The forts tend to draw on local reenactment units for participants as well as for help in maintaining the fort.

A **timeline event** includes more than just Civil War. Really big events, such as the River of Time in Bay City, Michigan, draw reenactors ranging from 1700s-era voyageurs to 1880s loggers. World War II reenactors often pair up with Civil War events, such as Parker's Crossroads, Tennessee.

A **naval reenactment** may represent fighting at sea with scale models or more modern full-size sailboats. There are models of ironclads, such as the C.S.S. *Virginia* and U.S.S. *Monitor,* that from a distance look amazingly real.

A **farbfest** is a Civil War event held in conjunction with another festival or craft fair. As this is a good opportunity to come into

Sea battles may involve only a few participants while providing historical reenactments for hundreds of spectators.

contact with a lot of the public, the recruiting of reenactors becomes more important than the reenacting itself. There is usually some drilling and a skirmish or two.

A **living history** is the reenactors' code phrase for a small-scale event. A living history can take place at a historic site, village, park or school. For a school living history, a tent or two may be set up outside. A number of reenactment items are spread out on a blanket for use in demonstrations. There is usually no overnight camping as there is with all the other types of reenactments.

WHY REENACT?

Certainly the mystique of the 1860s, where duty and honor were important, attracts a large number of people. The heritage that is kept alive at a reenactment is an important one. The act of preserving history in a living way fulfills an obligation that many feel. Many reenactors have researched the personal histories of their ancestors who fought in the war. Displaying that knowledge by role-playing a family member's life brings a special touch of poignancy to an individual's reenactment experience.

"My great-great-great uncle was with the Ohio Volunteer Militia. His regiment was mustered into the United States Army and fought at First Bull Run. He saw many important battles, yet he survived the war. My mother still has his diary and let me copy it. I study it, and when I do a reenactment I try to feel the things he felt when he was fighting the real battle. There are details in the diary that are not in any history books. In it are the discomforts and boredom of camp life, as well as the terror he felt over the prospect of a cannonball taking off his leg."

Some of the bravest and most daring exploits of American history took place during the War Between the States. In 1861 the Congressional Medal of Honor was created as a medal for the United States Navy and was soon expanded to include the United States Army. It became our nation's highest military honor. Some of the most noble words ever spoken were Abraham Lincoln's defense of the "great civil war" in the Gettysburg Address.

At night around the campfire, the stories revive the excitement. The joys and tears are pulled out with song and music. When the reverie of the night is silenced, only the rustle of hay under wool blankets can be heard while people sleep in rows of white canvas tents.

Come sit around the campfire as we relate the experience of these battles. Relive the marches and fall in for an inspection of this grand hobby. And, if the ladies are up for it, let's turn a toe and promenade on the dance floor of an elegant ballroom and bask in the high society of the 1860s.

Researching ancestors' histories and role playing their lifestyle brings a special poignancy to the reenactment experience.

A widow kneels at the grave site of a fallen ancestor in a special memorial service.

A Confederate enjoys the comfort of a campfire after a long day's battle with the mud and rain.

Contents of a Southern officer's haversack.

Fighting for the Confederacy

METHOD REENACTING

Reenactors often talk among themselves about how they get ready for the weekend. There is a lot of packing—not just putting things into the car—but detailed preparation of lots of little stuff. The haversack needs to contain the kinds of belongings that a Southern soldier would have had in it: knife, fork, spoon, plate, coffee beans, hardtack, Bible, letter-writing paper and a pencil. Cartridges need to be rolled, filled with powder for the battle, and packed into the cartridge box. Caps are loaded into the cap pouch. The gun is cleaned and oiled. Extra food is put in the forage box. A dozen other details are checked and rechecked. Roger's Rangers rule number one, "Don't forget nothing," echoes in the Confederate reenactor's head as his mind slips into history.

"I wish I owned a factory. Maybe if I were rich I would want to pass laws that would make me richer," a Confederate explains to a group of school kids. "I'd probably do it the same way the North does it. Instead of charging my neighbors more for my products, I would make it more expensive for people far away. People I don't even know could make me richer. But since I don't own a factory, I'm here to tell you that I'm gonna fight to make a new country, where people don't tell us what we're gonna have to pay for goods we need. I'm not gonna work hard in my fields to make some Northern factory owner rich."

Prisoners are rounded up by the Federal troops at a reenactment. At rifle point they are seated in front of a crowd of spectators.

"Why are you fighting?" one of the U.S. Army soldiers asks.

"We're fighting for our rights: states' rights, the right of secession, the right of citizens to determine their own future. We're fighting for our homes and families." Even if it's only for a weekend, the reenactor feels like he is going off to battle.

This is the process of "getting into it" that transforms a twentieth-century resident into that other time period. Maybe a drama student would call it "method reenacting." The soul of the individual begins to change. It's much more than going out to play soldier. The heart beats differently. Vision seems clearer and more intent. Passion takes the place of reason. Echoes of music swirl in the mind.

Arriving at the reenactment early for school day, the soldier steps out of the twentieth century and into his character for his demonstration. This is a preplanned ten- or fifteen-minute presentation to each group of students. Demonstrations include history of the period and topics such as uniforms, weapons, camps, blacksmithing, music, cavalry, artillery, medicine or transportation. The same demonstration may be given ten or more times in a day.

An arbor shade makes life in a summer encampment bearable.

BONNIE BLUE FLAG

We are a band of brothers, and native to the soil,
Fighting for our Liberty, with treasure, blood, and toil;
And when our rights were threatened, the cry rose near and far,
Hurrah for the Bonnie Blue Flag that bears a Single Star!

CHORUS (repeat after each verse):
Hurrah! Hurrah! For Southern rights Hurrah!
Hurrah! For the Bonnie Blue Flag that bears a single star.

As long as the Union was faithful to her trust,
Like friends and brethren kind were we, and just;
But now, when Northern treachery attempts our rights to mar,
We hoist on high the Bonnie Blue Flag that bears a single star.

First, gallant South Carolina nobly made the stand,
Then came Alabama and took her by the hand;
Next, quickly, Mississippi, Georgia, and Florida,
All raised on high the Bonnie Blue Flag that bears a single star.

Ye men of valor, gather 'round the banner of the right,
Texas and fair Louisiana join us in the fight;
With Davis, our loved President, and Stephens, statesmen rare
We'll rally round the Bonnie Blue Flag that bears the single star.

And here's to brave Virginia, the Old Dominion State,
With the young Confederacy at length has linked her faith;
Impelled by her example, now other states prepare
To hoist on high the Bonnie Blue Flag that bears a single star.

Then cheer, boys, cheer, raise a joyous shout
For Arkansas and North Carolina now have both gone out,
And let another rousing cheer for Tennessee be given,
The single star of the Bonnie Blue Flag has grown to be eleven.

Then here's to our Confederacy, strong we are and brave,
Like patriots of old we'll fight, our heritage to save;
And rather than submit to same, to die we would prefer,
So cheer for the Bonnie Blue Flag that bears a single star.

Keeping the battalion flag visible is important to morale and an honor for the soldier carrying it.

THE TARIFF ISSUE

Since Alexander Hamilton's Report on Manufactures to Congress in 1791, there had been increasing sentiment in the North toward protectionism. Protectionism means protecting a country's products by imposing a tariff on imported goods, making imported goods more expensive. The country's products would have a competitive advantage over foreign products. For the manufacturing North, this meant protecting the industries that existed there. For the agricultural South, protectionism meant higher prices on goods that it imported from Europe. The South was subjected to the control of a Congress that would impose tariffs as it felt necessary to ensure a strong manufacturing economy. In the North, it was felt that industrial independence was indispensable to political independence.

As most of the manufacturing occurred in the North, this benefited the North and hurt the South. An agricultural Southerner considered this unfair discrimination. Southern ports such as New Orleans, Savannah and Charleston thrived on the export of agricultural goods. The returning ships could bring the finest of wares from Europe, but Southerners were forced to pay an often-heavy tariff on those wares.

From the Tariff Act of 1816, the tariffs grew to an average of about thirty percent on goods such as textiles, paper, leather, hats, cabinetry, wool, glassware, hemp products, iron and lead products. One of the tariffs was even known as the Tariff of Abominations, and Southern politicians argued bitterly against the tariffs. The Yankee manufacturer was perceived as the evil that brought about this situation.

By December of 1860, South Carolina had had enough and resolved to remove itself from the United States. As there was no prohibition against this in the Constitution, South Carolina felt it had the legal right to secede. Its new flag was the Bonnie Blue Flag. Other southern states soon left the Union, creating the Confederate States of America.

Burning a building at this reenactment symbolizes the devastation caused by Sherman's march through the South.

A captured Confederate soldier says, "Because you're here. You're invading my land. I'm protecting my home and my family. Someday we're going to bring this war to *your* backyard."

"Don't tell that Yankee nothing," another rebel interrupts, as if there are secrets being given away.

"At least you can tell me what town you Seventh Tennessee boys are from."

"Lebanon," he says trying to hide his New Jersey accent. He knows where he is supposed to be from, even though he is a reenactor from Trenton.

At this reenactment in Hamilton, New Jersey, most of the Confederates are from north of the Mason-Dixon line, but they have galvanized for the weekend, meaning they have changed from Northerners to Southerners to balance the needs of this event. They are Lebanon Greys. In their minds they are farmers defending their land. Through the misfortunes of war they have been captured and are headed for a prison camp. They play the part of disgruntled prisoners well.

Almost all regiments in the Confederacy were named for the states in which they were assembled. A company was raised from a particular area or town. Many of the soldiers knew each other from civilian life. In reenacting, most soldiers join an association of people who represent a particular historical company, such as the Louisiana 7th Regiment, Company K. They may also be known for their town, such as the Covington Rifles. Reenactment companies are raised from an area or town for convenience. It is easy to decide which reenactments to attend if the members live near each other. The tradition of the particular unit represented by the reenactors is reinforced by the regional character of the organization.

"Let the generals worry about the war. I'm a private soldier, and I just want to keep myself dry and my rifle clean." There's no way to tell what this person does in real life. His uniform is torn and patched. There's dirt and dust of every description on it. His hat looks like it's been sat on a hundred times, as was the practice during the war: sitting on the hat instead

Defending their camp from behind a pile of logs, these soldiers take careful aim.

Out of the early morning mist the cavalry rides to support the infantry.

The battle for the top of the hill is costly but critical.

of the ground kept the soldier's backside dry. The soldier roughly reformed the hat when it was time to get up, and eventually, it became slouched; hence, its name.

Some affluent reenactors find satisfaction in portraying common soldiers. A doctor, lawyer, or architect in real life becomes a private in the army. It is a great stress-reliever to change hats for a couple of days.

"I'm a farmer. Sometimes it seems like we're gonna starve to death, even without this war," a Confederate explains. "I left my wife and children to defend our rights, but now I don't know what that means. It seems like we're fighting a rich man's war to protect their property. My wife writes me that she has to work harder than ever."

CONFEDERATE DRESSING

"I'd like to try reenacting," a spectator confides to some soldiers in camp. A dozen eyes light up and the reenactors start coming out with uniform pieces and leather accessories.

"We're Confederate today, but you can still wear these Federal sky-blue pants. You can imagine you got them in a raid on a supply train."

"Or, maybe off a dead Yank," another soldier jokes.

"Don't worry, they're clean. If they seem a little itchy, it's because they're wool. You'll get used to it."

"You can try my gray wool shell jacket. I don't need it since I got my jean-cloth one," another says as each soldier lends a different piece of uniform to the beginner.

"Before you put the jacket on, you need this muslin shirt. It's like a Civil War underwear shirt."

"Here are my old brogans. You'll look like a real Confederate in these boots."

"Put this strap over your left shoulder. This is your cartridge box. Over your right shoulder goes your haversack. I use it for Seminole War-era events, but it's right for Confederates too."

"You can wear this U.S. belt upside down. That means it's captured. U.S. upside down

This Southern reenactor guards the breastworks.

A foot soldier wearing a jean-cloth jacket takes a momentary rest from the heat of the battle.

The differences in Southern uniforms are noted as these men gather around an early morning fire for warmth and conversation.

The chaplain prays over the troops before the battle begins.

kind of looks likes s. n. That can mean Southern Nation if you want. The waist belt goes around everything to hold it all together while you're running. That cap pouch slides a little over to your right."

"Here, I bet this forage cap will fit you. It's federal blue, but that's okay, a lot of Confederates wore blue pieces with their uniforms."

This is how most reenactors get started.

They use a few borrowed pieces, put together spontaneously. This is when the reenacting bug bites hardest. If there is a spare rifle and the recruit marches into battle with the unit, there is hardly anything that will stop him from coming back for more.

Reenactors put a lot of research into their uniforms and accouterments. Their first purchase is usually the sky-blue pants of the

Standards among Confederate clothing can be seen among this general and his staff.

An example of this is Hays' Brigade, consisting of several regiments, including the 5th, 6th, 7th, 8th and 14th Louisiana. They were attached to the Army of Northern Virginia. Some of the individual companies had specified their own uniforms, but by the battle of Sharpsburg (Antietam), their old uniforms were worn out, and most were wearing Richmond Depot-supplied shell jackets of jean cloth. Jean cloth is a material of cross-woven cotton and wool, which was a predecessor of today's blue jeans. The cotton in the Civil War jean cloth was usually natural white, while the wool was dyed gray or butternut. Butternut ranged from tan to a dark brown with a green cast and was a common tinting agent for wool. Even jackets made totally from wool were often shades of butternut. Reenactors may have several Confederate uniforms to properly represent the different time periods of the war.

United States Army. Confederates commonly wore these pants, so they are suitable for either Northerners or Southerners.

The South had a great variety of infantry uniforms, due to the regional character of their organization. Particularly early in the war, the local militia units made up their own uniforms and showed up in parade-ground splendor. After a few clashes, some of these uniforms were recognized as impractical. When the uniforms were worn out, they were replaced by whatever depot was supplying the theater they served.

To revive the spirits of kindred dead who fought for their land and livelihood is a great spiritual experience for thousands of people today. It enables a bond with ancestors that cannot be achieved any other way. This is the passion of reenacting that keeps people involved for decades. They are proud to wear the Confederate uniform and travel to a time not too far distant.

A battalion poses for a picture in front of the tunnel at Tunnel Hill, Georgia.

A Confederate navy man has done a lot of research to be sure his clothing is authentic.

In the quiet hours of
night, the loneliness of
being away from loved
ones sets in deep.

The splendor and the agony of reenactment are both visible in this battle scene.

Guns firing by battalion is a spectacular sight.

Preserving the Union

SETTING UP CAMP

"Hey, Bob. You made it early," a fellow unit member says as Bob pulls up to Union camp. "Let's get ya unloaded so you can clear your car out of camp. Rally 'round boys; everybody grab something."

Glad for the help, Bob responds, "I'll unlock the trunk."

"The company street is along this string they laid out," one of the unit's sergeants says. "We gotta get real tight because they expect a lot of soldiers here. Where's your tent stakes?"

"In the Waterlift Arsenal box, the one labeled 'Enfield.'"

"Get those poles from the roof of Bob's car and let's get this tent up."

Tink, tink, tink, tink, and the stakes are driven into the ground through the tent loops while the canvas is squared. As soon as the tent is staked, one of the privates walks the ridge-pole into the tent and the white canvas begins to

A Federal sailor beats the bass drum as he marches to raise the Union flag.

In the morning hours, Federal troops prepare for the afternoon battle.

dance like a fidgety ghost. A tent pole is passed inside and the other pole is attached. The ghost stops dancing and the wedge tent is rigid and ready. Bob finishes unloading his car and says, "Hey, yuz guys, thanks."

There is more happening here than what meets the eye. It isn't just a tent being pitched but an individual getting into character and merging with the unit. For some reason, unloading the car, unrolling white canvas tents, pounding stakes and setting up camp is a prerequisite.

"I've come in late to an event before because I had to work late or something. If I arrive Saturday morning instead of Friday night, I feel like I'm out of step, and it doesn't happen right," a veteran reenactor confides. "I don't know exactly why, but I just can't step into a firing line and feel like a soldier."

The authentic camps are simple and are set up in an orderly fashion along company streets. A dog tent—a pair of shelter halves buttoned together—is the Civil War version of the pup tent. It sleeps two and barely keeps them out of the rain. The A-frame, or wedge tent, is the most common and can sleep up to six people. The private's tent requires only three poles to set up: a ridgepole that goes across the top and a pole at both ends to hold up the ridgepole.

The details inside the tent help bring a reenactor's individual scene to life. Hay is scattered across the bottom of the tent, providing

a dry, comfortable bed. A ground cloth is laid over the hay, and several layers of wool blankets are spread out. Food is stored in the forage box. Several ammunition boxes disguise the necessities of life while creating an image of life in the war. More props include a folding stool or two, reproduction Civil War-era newspapers, and uniform accouterments strewn about the tent floor.

Sometimes a fly is erected as a sunshade. This is a ten- or twelve-foot-square piece of canvas with grommets along the edges. Six to ten poles and guy ropes are required to keep it up. This can serve as a front porch to a tent. Canvas flies were common in extended encampments during the war, but for campaigning, only the highest-ranking officers would go to the trouble of having them set up.

All around the field site, preparations are being made for tomorrow's battle.

"I think we'll move the battery from behind the trees, so let's get a tractor to move your stuff in," an event coordinator tells the artillery crew.

"It'll be hard for us to work around there with all that tall grass," the battery commander complains.

"Don't worry, we'll have that area cleared out for you by this afternoon. The mower is just about finished with bush hogging the back end of Confederate camp. We have a lot more coming than we thought, and it looks like we're gonna have to make room for them. Soon as he's finished, I'll get him down in your area. We can tow your cannon down there now. The tractor is freed up. He just finished spotting the Ohio battery next to where you'll be."

The event coordinator wants to make everybody happy and adds as part of his sales pitch, "You know, we had so many sutlers show up that we had to start angling them off the road. Should be good shopping for you!"

"Did ya get that water hose run down to the Union cavalry picket line?" the coordinator says to one of his helpers.

"Yea, we finished that about an hour ago. Ran most of the line through bushes so nobody can see it."

Camp life is sometimes
confined to small spaces.

GETTING INTO THE SPIRIT

The intoxicating scent of burning wood permeates the air as the first campfires are lit. The wind gets a little cooler as dusk approaches. The slamming of car doors is replaced by the murmur of a hundred conversations. Strains of music are heard and everyone gets into the feeling of reenactment by thinking about what an actual Union soldier would have thought about. For the Union man, it's the spirit of '76. Patriots of old are revitalized in the soldier's mind as he recalls the citizens who founded this country and fought the Revolutionary War. Sentiments of loyalty fill the breast of the soldier as pride of country rises to a lump in his throat.

"Lincoln has put over one hundred thousand troops into the field. In this camp, there are boys from all over the Union," a reenactor says as he puts himself into the mind-set of a

Civilian women volunteer to
cook for the men to make
times a little easier.

33

The cavalry adds flair and fast excitement to sometimes slow battles.

A moment to read.

soldier in the Civil War. "I met soldiers from Maine to Michigan today. How wonderful it is we can march together for freedom the way our forefathers did in 1776."

"The thought of someone wanting to tear apart the most glorious country on earth is unthinkable," a reenactor responds, as if it were a current issue in his consciousness.

To go beyond the superficial and really reenact requires a mental discipline based on knowledge of history. Libraries and bookstores become the watering holes of learning. The longer a person is a reenactor, the more books he acquires. One time he might search for different types of hats, another time for ways soldiers buttoned their jackets. How tents are set up, what style of shoes were worn, and whether soldiers rolled up their sleeves are just a few subjects of individual investigative odysseys. Research keeps people motivated all year long so that when the big events come along, the reenactors are eager to incorporate their new knowledge into their accouterments and character roles.

When the troops have downtime, rifles are stacked and ready for quick access.

BECOMING THE CHARACTER

One method used by reenactors to get into and sustain character is meditation or mind experiments. It can start as a simple daydream. Through this method, some even claim to transcend their experience of life and enter another world of time.

People who achieve this the best are those who practice the method year-round. "When I'm bored at work, I can conjure a daydream just by looking out over trees where no power lines run through. It looks like a nineteenth-century scene," says a reenactor who drafts for a living.

Three generations of reenactors from Georgia have galvanized and become Federal for the weekend at the Battle of Resaca, Georgia.

Union pride.

In confronting a twentieth-century situation in daily life, a reenactor might use a mental exercise to find a resolution. For instance, he imagines how Grant or Sherman would have handled the same situation.

Sometimes mentally calling a conference of great leaders helps to tackle a difficult problem. "I run a business. The only people who know as much as I do about my business are my competitors, and I'm not about to ask them for answers," confides a senior reenactor. "So I call a roundtable conference in my mind. I tell my secretary to hold all calls and not to disturb me. Then I close my eyes and imagine sitting at the head of the table in an important room. I welcome all the usual participants.

"'President Lincoln, it's so good to see you again. Please, sit down. General Grant, General Sherman, Mr. Stanton, I have some questions for discussion.' Then I proceed with my mental conference. It seems as if they are really there. I don't know if their spirits have actually come into my consciousness, but they advise me that way. Some of my best business decisions have been the result of their guidance."

Reenactors' feelings about the great leaders of the Civil War approach hero worship. At night in the camp, looking at the same stars that Lincoln gazed upon, a reenactor feels a kinship with glory. There is a reverence for the accomplishments of men who achieved greatness in a time that demanded greatness. Over time, we have given these men even greater glorification, and reenactors try to emulate the attributes that made their heroes great.

The hours around the campfire can be joyous and full of laughter and song or quiet and pensive.

A wedge tent set up on the historical Lakeview Docks of Wildwood Crest, New Jersey.

ESPOUSING THE UNION CAUSE

"In a lot of ways, John Brown started the War," a Union soldier explains to a group of school kids who were bussed in to see the reenactment at Resaca, Georgia. "He was an abolitionist—that's someone who wants to abolish, or do away with, slavery. John Brown attempted to lead a violent overthrow of slavery. He started with the seizure of several buildings at Harper's Ferry in 1859. There was an arsenal there, and he planned to distribute the arms to the slaves. He was captured by a group of U.S. soldiers, including Lt. Colonel Robert E. Lee. John Brown was tried and hung for treason, thus becoming a martyr of the abolitionist cause.

"'John Brown's Body' was one of the most popular marching songs of the United States Army and helped inspire many people to enlist. A host of soldiers joined the army to free the slaves. This was particularly true of the Black American soldiers, including the

Infantry from the 54th Massachusetts take a lunch break at the Battle of Franklin, Tennessee.

JOHN BROWN'S BODY

John Brown's body lies a-mouldering in the grave.
John Brown's body lies a-mouldering in the grave.
John Brown's body lies a-mouldering in the grave.
His soul is marching on.

CHORUS (repeat after each verse):
Glory, glory, hallelujah.
Glory, glory, hallelujah.
Glory, glory, hallelujah.
His soul is marching on.

He's gone to be a soldier in the army of the Lord.
He's gone to be a soldier in the army of the Lord.
He's gone to be a soldier in the army of the Lord.
His soul is marching on.

John Brown's knapsack is strapped upon his back.
John Brown's knapsack is strapped upon his back.
John Brown's knapsack is strapped upon his back.
His soul is marching on.

John Brown died that the slaves might be free.
John Brown died that the slaves might be free.
John Brown died that the slaves might be free.
His soul is marching on.

The stars above in heaven now are looking kindly down.
The stars above in heaven now are looking kindly down.
The stars above in heaven now are looking kindly down
On the grave of ol' John Brown.

famous 54th Massachusetts."

"I don't own slaves," proclaims a soldier portraying a member of the 54th at Olustee. "I can't imagine anyone in Boston owning slaves. I don't think it's right. This is supposed to be a free country, and I don't see how it can be free if some people are owned by others."

A New Hampshire reenactor tells his story, "It was about the time of John Brown's capture of Harper's Ferry that we organized a militia group in our town. Several people had

Fife and drum corps from Fort Douglas, Utah, adds music to all the reenactments it attends.

Two ships reenact an 1862 sea battle of the CSS *Alabama* that terrorized the East Coast.

Union sailors prepare to defend their ship from a Confederate attack at Wildwood Crest, New Jersey.

seen service in the Mexican War, so we elected them as our officers. Many 'Southrons' view Lincoln as an abolitionist. I know he believes slavery is wrong, but I think he feels it is more wrong for states to leave the Union. They can't do it and we won't let them."

Besides making all men free, there were many other reasons for helping to preserve these United States. When a reenactor talks to spectators, he or she can give personal reasons for joining the army.

"All my friends joined the 57th Indiana," says a Louisiana reenactor who is Federal this weekend at Selma, Alabama. "Most of the boys in my company went to Sunday school with me. I never would have guessed we could be sitting this far from home. It makes me miss the work around the farm. Still I'm glad I'm here."

Maintaining the Union is a concept well understood by nationalistic citizens. The patriotic stirrings of our forefathers dwell in the hearts of many. "I still remember the rally," recounts an easterner. "They had speaker after speaker on a platform giving speeches. Pretty girls were waving flags. There was a great big banner that urged all men of the Union to join the army. Finally, I couldn't stand it any more. I rushed up and signed my name. They gave me a muster sheet and, boy, did I feel proud. They fed us a real good meal, and then a uniformed man who became our colonel marched us to a field with a bunch of tents. That's how I started in the army. You want some of this?" and the reenactor tries to pass a piece of hardtack to a spectator.

"I joined the army to kill Johnny Rebs, but all we do is march around Minnesota looking for Indians and battling flies," says a reenactor playing the part of a disgruntled soldier. "I thought I would get to go back east, but I haven't been east of Mankato, thanks to the Sioux uprising. It seems these Indians want their own separate country, too."

"I come from Ireland," a reenactor says in an accent whose realism took years to achieve. "I could have gotten a job with the factories, but those cities make me feel so closed in. They gave me one hundred dollars in cash money to join the regiment. That's a fortune. I get paid every month and I'm saving that. When I get out, they promised me enough land to start a farm. I'll be sitting pretty when this war is over."

Not all who joined the army did so voluntarily. The Enrollment Act of 1863 was passed to draft men into the army and bolster lagging enlistments. It was not well received, as most of those men with patriotic stirrings had already volunteered.

"It's a rich man's war," gripes a reenactor. "If I had three hundred dollars, I'd buy my way out of the draft. At the rate the swamps are sending men to heaven by way of the hospital tent, I probably would be buying my life."

A reenactor with strong Southern sympathies but who is assigned to play a Yankee may take the character of a drafted soldier. This is a popular United States Army impression in the South where there aren't enough real Federals

Naval personnel sign for their meager but much-needed pay.

to field a believable number of loyal troops.

"I got drafted. I don't wish to be here, and I've thought of running, but I don't want to get shot. They shoot deserters, you know." Then the Mississippi reenactor breaks out of character and confides to the spectators listening, "Actually they didn't have enough Federals for this weekend, so our whole unit is wearing the blue suit. Everybody's got to take turns. Nobody *wants* to be a Yankee."

Federal Zouaves from New York strike dashing figures. Modeled after the French colonial service, they were famous for marksmanship, precision drill, and colorful uniforms.

DRESSING FOR THE PART

"Private soldiers' uniforms are practical," explains Captain Charlie Tarbox at the Battlefield Bed and Breakfast in Gettysburg. Charlie gives daily demonstrations after breakfast and is very good at it. "Each piece of gear has a purpose." Charlie picks a volunteer and begins to dress her as a soldier.

"First, you get a dark blue sack coat and hat. You should be wearing sky-blue pants, but I won't make you put them on. A marching soldier has to carry sleeping gear. This includes a gum blanket—a rubber-coated piece of canvas that a soldier can spread upon the ground for his bed. It keeps him dry from the bottom. If he is lucky and has two, he can use the other as a cover and keep the rain off. The gum doubles as a poncho for marching in the rain and carries a lot of things when wrapped in a roll and tied around him.

"In that roll might be a tick, which is a man-sized canvas bag that can be stuffed with leaves or straw to make a mattress for the night. In the morning the tick is emptied and rolled into the gum. A blanket is in the roll, as

Before the Battle of Franklin, Tennessee, a Federal soldier sits atop the breastwork and writes a letter home to his loved ones.

is any extra clothing the soldier has.

"For water, a soldier has a tin canteen, usually covered in wool. The wool serves as an insulator. On a hot day the wool covering is wetted and the water evaporates off the wool, cooling the water inside, much like sweat cools a human.

"Food is carried in a haversack. Normal ration is for three days. A well-supplied Union soldier might have hardtack, meat, dried vegetables and a few personal items.

"Ammunition for an infantryman's musket is separated in two places: the cartridge box and the cap pouch attached to a waist belt. In the cartridge box are up to forty cartridges. A cartridge consists of a lead ball and gunpowder wrapped and tied in paper. The soldier pulls the cartridge out of the box and tears it open with his teeth. He then dumps gunpowder down the barrel and pushes the ball down with the musket's ramrod. The cap pouch holds the caps that ignite the powder. He places a cap over the nipple of a percussion musket in preparation for firing.

"Also attached to the waist belt is a frog that holds a bayonet. The bayonet's primary purpose is as a sharp weapon to be attached to the forward end of a musket and thrust into an enemy. But the bayonet can hold a rifle upside down in the rain when stuck into the ground. Two muskets thrust upside down into the ground on their bayonets can hold a string to support shelter halves or to serve as a clothesline for drying clothes. When separated from the rifle, the bayonet can be a candleholder or a digging tool."

Captain Tarbox salutes and says, "Let's have a round of applause for our volunteer and go outside for a rifle-firing demonstration."

Drummers have an important role in keeping the men marching forward.

Branches of the Armies

These four infantrymen came from the Czech Republic to spend their vacation time fighting for Waul's Texas Legion.

There are a number of things that are the same for Confederates and Federals in reenacting. For one, because both armies originally shared the same origin, their organization and weaponry are similar.

INFANTRY

"George, what's the best deal you can give me on a musket package?" a new reenactor asks the Regimental Quartermaster inside his big, white marquee tent. "I need everything—a Springfield, the sling, bayonet, frog and my basic tools. I better get some caps and a couple cans of powder, too."

Over on the table are stacks of reproduction muskets, still in their cardboard packing. George looks through the pile, finds the Springfield and gives it to the novice before he starts talking about the price. With gun in hand, the recruit starts imagining what it will be like to use it in battle. George knows that

The infantry is impressive in the uniforms of the Union.

A soldier from the 125th Ohio V.I. relaxes between battles.

handling the weapon will sell it. With eyes glazed, the customer hands over his Master Card, no longer concerned with the cost. A bag of extras is passed to the recruit and he walks off with his rifle toward camp.

"Oooooweee, a brand new rifle. Lookee here, fellas. The boy is serious," and the initiation begins with a little poking of fun. "Let me put my blinders on—that barrel is so shiny."

"What's in that 'farby' paper bag?" Another old soldier takes the bag and starts to display its contents. "A brand new leather sling. That's gonna hurt; it's as stiff as a board. This bayonet is so bright I think we can signal with it." He angles it off the sun and gets someone a few tents down in the eye with its reflection. "And look at this—hundreds of caps and two pounds of powder. Get ready to roll some cartridges, boys."

Not wanting to lose the recruit, the captain strolls over before it goes too far. "Put these tools in the bottom half of the tins in

LONG ARMS

The infantry's main weapons were muskets or rifles, known as infantry long arms or shoulder arms. They were quite varied during the time of the war. In the beginning, many of the militia units marched with whatever muskets they had on hand. Flintlock muskets fired round lead balls or whatever could be stuffed down the barrel of the muzzle-loaded weapon.

Rifling a bore put grooves into the bore of the gun to spin the load, producing a more accurate weapon. The elongated ball or minié ball gave the firearms greater range. Percussion muskets started to be seen in the 1830s, but early in the war there were not enough to go around.

Mississippi rifles were leftover from the Mexican War in the late 1840s and found early service.

The Enfield and Springfield rifles were two of the more prevalent shoulder arms as the war progressed. Each had a number of variations and improvements. As their use became widespread, the .57-, .577-, and .58-caliber minié balls started to become standards of ammunition. This eased supply problems by reducing the number of different types of cartridges that were required for a battle. Toward the end of the war, breechloaders and multiple-shot rifles, such as the Henry, were seen more often.

your cartridge box or they'll end up buried in the hay. That's a mighty fine rifle, son. I bet these boys will help you make it look like it's been around a while."

Like kids with a new toy, they gather around to give the lad some advice. "Ya wanna blue or brown the barrel?"

"I like brown. Looks older—like *my* rifle," offers a veteran.

"No one below the rank of sergeant is allowed to carry a pistol," an officer bellows, as if there were some kind of test required to buy sergeant stripes. "You privates go stash them in your tents. Olustee has made rules to prevent privates from carrying pistols."

There is a safety concern with reproduction pistols. When loaded for firing a live round, balls hold the black powder in each

A young color bearer carries the Confederate flag in battle, helping bolster the infantry's enthusiasm.

chamber of the revolver. When a pistol is loaded for a reenactment, no ball holds the black powder in the chamber. There is a danger that one cylinder in firing might ignite another, creating what is known as a chain fire. But because pistols are inexpensive, most reenactors have at least one.

There are few instruction manuals on how to reenact. Most of the practical information is handed down around campfires or while visiting at each other's houses between events. It's at these times that even hard-core reenactors drop their nineteenth-century personas and take time to instruct initiates. Skills such as rifle cleaning and cartridge rolling are best taught one-on-one.

When instructed in company or battalion, everyone is in persona. That doesn't mean the sergeants turn into a nightmare version of a marine drill sergeant. If they did, their units wouldn't last long. Instead, leaders play the role of gentlemen who are working with their men to draw the best out of them. In units that have been around a while, an attitude of mutual respect has developed.

"Donnie Barrett is more than an officer; he cares about his people and works with them. When asking for something to be done, he says please. If things are right, he gives compliments. At those times when people need to be corrected, he does it in a low tone of voice

In grand numbers, the Federal infantry marches against the Confederate lines in the Battle of Nashville.

Overrunning a Confederate position can be exhausting and leave behind a pattern of devastation.

away from other people and still smiles."

"Fire by company, ready, aim, fire!" and thirty guns go off at once. This doesn't happen without a lot of practice. After assembling for colors in the morning, companies drill on facing movements, manual of arms, marching and firing. The more battles the unit attends, the more the drills can be put into practice.

"Company, forward, guide right, march!" shouts the captain, and the troops begin

doing what soldiers have done since ancient times.

"Right wheel, march!" causes the company to pivot, changing their direction of march.

"Forward, march!" straightens the worm movement of men into a straight path.

"By company, into line, march!" and a dozen different movements take place in a complicated maneuver as the men are made ready to wage war.

Roaring cannons and musket volleys make

The signal corps sends the general's orders to the distant artillery.

rifles going off at one time. This type of coordination is impracticable with a voice command.

Most of us have an image of boys doing the drumming, but all ages were drummers during the war. Communication was a critical task, but the field music also had a morale-building effect. The drum kept everyone in step and helped build the feeling of unity in the hearts of those marching to battle.

"I also drum for a country band, and it's amazing how much this military drumming has helped my ability. Knowing all these rudiments really improves my competence in other styles of music," says a gray-haired Confederate.

Playing a fife is somewhat difficult and requires a lot of practice. Yet, the number of fifers has been growing in the past few years, and their level of expertise has greatly increased.

ARTILLERY

The cannons are handled by the artillery branch of the army. Heavy artillery are the big guns: 24-pounders, 32-pounders and 11-inch mortars that are most associated with forts or siege situations.

"I love it when we fire that big 32-pounder at Old Fort Jackson in Savannah. Everyone wants to take a turn at pulling the lanyard to shoot it. You should hear the echo off the water when it's fired—it burns a pound of

it almost impossible to hear orders shouted on the battlefield. To get an order passed to a company, a drummer and possibly a fifer are needed. Every unit would like to have a drummer and fifer, and their services are actively sought after. Incentives include the unit purchase of instruments or even lessons.

For example, the command "fire on the drum" causes a group of riflemen to fire at exactly the same time. The drum call has three parts: the first two parts get everyone ready to fire; the final roll signals for everyone to fire on the final beat. In actual combat, this would unleash a sheet of lead toward the enemy. In a reenactment, it causes a roar from dozens of

A few lucky artillerymen catch a ride on a limber.

powder. We've got the same gun that was used in the movie *Glory* at Battery Wagner. Soon we will have two working 32-pounders."

The field, or light, artillery are the ones most often seen on the battlefield. Light artillery means mobile artillery. The cannon and its ammunition can be drawn by horses to the places where it is needed in a changing battle situation.

Variations of field artillery include the Parrott gun, or 10-pounder; the Napoleon, or M1857 gun howitzer; and the three-inch ordnance rifle, or Rodman. They can be made of iron or bronze. The mountain howitzer is commonly used in reenactments because it is small. Little mortars, known as Cohern mortars, are sometimes used by artillery units.

Field artillery pieces are generally co-owned by a group of private reenactors. They often form a corporation for the purpose of protecting their very large investment. The field-artillery cannon is a large gun, mounted on a carriage. The limber is a two-wheeled wagon used for hauling ammunition that attaches to the cannon carriage. The caisson is a short ammunition wagon. To bring the entire rig to a reenactment site requires one or more trailers. Some reenactment units have horses to bring the piece into battle, and they must be trailered as well.

"So far, our unit has a Cohern mortar and a mountain howitzer. We want to get a limber together so we can do it right. We would like a caisson, too, but not many groups have them, so we don't feel bad about that. We just take it one step at a time. It's a lot of money, you know," says a member of a new unit.

The Washington Artillery from New Orleans marches in single file to their battery.

The guns must be in the right position and the firing precisely accurate so as not to waste powder.

The artillery and infantry join forces to hold the battle line.

With a precision that comes from years of experience, each man takes his position and waits for orders. The captain leans forward to his lieutenant and says, "Sir, would you please bring our battery to bear on those Yankees advancing upon us?"

"It would be my pleasure, sir," responds the lieutenant. "Sergeant, prepare to fire."

"Yes, sir." The sergeant then barks out the orders, and the men respond with the élan that comes from repeated drilling. As the men assume the ready-to-fire position, the sergeant requests permission to fire.

"You may fire at will, Sergeant," and the lieutenant's words are barely off his lips as the report of the cannon blasts across the battle-

Loud noise and plenty of smoke are common to the artillery crew as the battle rages on.

field. Automatically, the sergeant begins the reloading procedure.

The Washington Artillery is one of the most prestigious reenactment groups. The original military unit existed before the Civil War and still exists as a National Guard unit, having participated in Desert Storm. With a tradition like this to live up to, the members of this unit are extraordinarily concerned with historical accuracy. Their uniforms are impeccable and all match to a degree seldom seen in reenacting. They use a dark-gray wool with the red edging associated with the artillery. They also consistently win live-round target shoots, such as the annual Oak Alley event in Vacherie, Louisiana.

In the morning mist, the silent cannons of the South act as a meeting place for the commanders of both armies.

CAVALRY

Cavalry is the mounted branch of the army. Cavalry theory in the Civil War came from practical experience in the Napoleonic Wars. Riding on horses, the cavalry can act as the eyes of the army. They scout for the best roads, find forage or food for the army on the march, and look for the enemy. That is why the cavalry were often the first to clash when two armies were on the field in search of each other.

Most large reenactment battles start with dashing cavalry charges. Pistols and carbines are fired and sabers clang in this carefully orchestrated part of the battle. This is probably the most dangerous type of reenacting and is usually separated from the infantry fighting for safety reasons. But cavalry reenacting is the most glamorous and attracts many riders.

"I love horses. I've been raising and showing them since I was a kid," says a dedicated reenactor. "When I was young, the horses on the farm were my toys. When I got older and found out about reenacting, I could hardly believe I could go play army with my horses. You know, you have to ride your horse every day, so I hardly ever miss a weekend doing some kind of reenactment or living history. When I'm not doing Civil War, I do cowboy stuff. I can wear my Federal outfit and portray a cavalry soldier out of the Indian Wars, too. I even ride in some parades."

Many Southern reenactors come from the country. It is no surprise that Southern reenactments field a lot of horses. This is in keeping with history. Some of the most effective cavalry the world had ever seen fought for the Confederacy. Just like General J. E. B. Stuart, many Southerners were reared in the saddle and were excellent horsemen. Like the cavalry reenactors of today, many Confederate cavalrymen brought their own horses to the war.

For a price, even the city dweller can reenact mounted cavalry. "I don't have time to take care of a horse," says a stockbroker. "But, I've got a stable that understands what I'm doing, and they take real good care of my mount. They ride him, feed him and brush

At the break of dawn, the men ready their horses for the day's ride.

CS CAVALRY HQ

The calvary charges into
battle to defend their
current position.

Sabers clash, hooves pound, and men scream as the cavalry engages in battle.

common for reenactors who do not own horses to fight as dismounted cavalry. To dismount and fight meant that one out of every four horsemen would hold four horses. The other three men would get off their horses and fire their carbines and pistols on foot. There was a particular drill for the fast, get-in-and-get-out type of fighting best exemplified by C.S.A. General Nathan Bedford Forrest's style of attack. He hit fast and hit hard. Many reenactors are inspired by this, and dismounted cavalry is growing in popularity.

"I live in Mobile and reenact at Fort Gaines a lot. They don't have a lot of room for horses, but we have a group that fights with dismounted cavalry drill. We're really good at it, and we look sharp. There's a lot of pride in that," touts a cavalryman.

"I used to fight as mounted cavalry, but my horse Gracie is getting a little too old. So I joined the Seventh U.S., and I can still wear all

him down every day. I even store my horse trailer there. It costs me hundreds a month, but that doesn't bother me. It's worth it to get out to a couple of events a month and ride."

Because of the romance of the cavalry, it is

RIDING A RAID

'Tis old Stonewall the Rebel that leans on his sword,
And while we are mounting prays low to the Lord:
"Now each cavalier that loves honor and right,
Let him follow the feather of Stuart tonight."

CHORUS (repeat after each verse):
Come tighten your girth and slacken your rein;
Come buckle your blanket and holster again;
Try the click of your trigger and balance your blade,
For he must ride sure that goes Riding a Raid!

Now gallop, now gallop to swim or to ford!
Old Stonewall, still watching, prays low to the Lord:
"Good-bye, dear old Rebel, the river's not wide,
And Maryland's lights in her window to guide."

There's a man in a white house with blood on his mouth!
If there's knaves in the North, there are braves in the South.
We are three thousand horses, and not one afraid;
We are three thousand sabers and not a dull blade.

Then gallop, then gallop by ravines and rocks!
Who would bar us the way take his toll in hard knocks;
For with these points of steel, on the line of Penn
We have made some fine strokes—and we'll make 'em again.

The cavalry rides like ghosts from the past.

my cavalry gear and fight with guns a-blazin'. My carbine is on a sling, and I can fire two pistols at once. We all fight like that. Boy, do we make an uproar. You can always spot us on the field by the racket we create. But we do it on foot, and we don't have to worry about the horses."

Whether on horse or on foot, the *esprit de corps* of cavalry attracts a large number of reenactors.

Two German citizens join the cavalry to ride for the South.

The tracks give this cannon mobility, allowing it to turn left and right with the help of a mighty tough crew.

Garrisoning the Fort

Ralph Oalmann repairs cars. His boss and customers in Mandeville, Louisiana, keep him very busy, but he tries to schedule his work not to interfere with his reenacting on weekends. Ralph has a nice house, and in the backyard a building contains his forge, blacksmithing tools and racks of raw stock. There's even a pile of first-rate coal.

On weeknights, Ralph's thick arms beat out orders. He makes lantern hangers and campfire tools modeled on museum examples and tent stakes till he doesn't want to look at them any more, and he does a lot of custom work. His favorite items are the decorative filigree pieces that are the hallmark of an artist in iron. His leaves are so delicate that if sprayed green they would look real. But Ralph prefers black, and he treats his metal with beeswax. This adds a touch of sweetness to the pungent, acrid smell of the burning coal and red-hot irons in the fire.

The inside of a powder chamber at Fort McHenry is illuminated by the afternoon light.

Blacksmith demonstrations are some of the most popular at fort reenactments and on sutlers' row. These hand-forged cooking tools are not only practical but also objects of art.

On Thursday night, he finishes his last bunch of tent stakes and gently puts them in his barrel, being careful not to mar their finish. He steps out into the Louisiana muck that gives the building its name, Muddy Forge. Opening the camper top, he slides the barrel into the back of his pickup.

After getting the rest of the special orders stowed, Ralph goes through the ritual of packing, always feeling like he's forgetting something. "I don't need the tent this time; I'm sleeping in the barracks," he mutters. "I've got enough blankets. Two shirts ought to be enough." Ralph has won contests for the authentic contents of his haversack, but checks it again just to make sure.

Before work the next morning, he kisses his wife good-bye for the weekend. "Fridays are always the longest, I hope they remember

I want to leave early," and he drives away down a picturesque rural road curtained with Spanish moss.

"Three o'clock, remember I'm outa here by three," he says to the only person who got there before he did.

"Got another reenactment, Ralph?"

"Yeah, Fort Gaines in Mobile," he answers as he opens his tool chest.

"Why don'tcha just move to Mobile? You're there every month."

Cars start coming in and everybody wants them finished by the weekend. Getting a little extra mileage out of Ralph, the boss dangles three o'clock like a carrot on a stick. They play this game every time Ralph wants off, so he puts in extra Saturdays between reenactments to make sure to get the time off when he needs it.

At a quarter to three, the boss lets off the pressure and says, "As soon as you've finished this one, you can go." Ralph is almost done anyway, and he takes the car out for its test drive. Everything is okay. He finishes the paperwork, and as the second hand sweeps around three o'clock, he's walking to the truck. He peeks in the back and tries to think if he's forgotten anything.

He knows the route by heart and never looks at a map. Reenactors learn the roads in surrounding states like most people know their hometowns. They are regulars at gas stations two states away. Ralph fills up at an exit in Alabama, where they treat him like a neighbor.

It's still daylight as he goes over the long bridge to Dauphin Island. He relaxes as he makes the final curves into Fort Gaines. The entrance, called the sally port, is open, and he drives right into the fort. A bunch of cars are already there, but the area by the blacksmith shop is open, so he parks next to it.

"Hey, Ralph," is repeated a dozen times as friends come over to see him.

"Well, I'm burning daylight," and Ralph excuses himself to finish unloading into the shop. Driving out, he parks far away from the entrance to allow plenty of room for the tourists to park. He gets into his uniform by the truck, and the click-click of his heel plates echo in the sally port as he walks back into the fort.

At the blacksmith shop he picks up his bedroll and walks it over to Officers' Quarters. He gathers up an armful of straw on the way in. The place is alive. A dozen people are making up bunks and another dozen are hanging around. "Ralph, there was a lot of competition for your bunk, but Melinda made us save it for you."

"Aw, thanks," he says in bashful tones, not wanting to press his advantage. As the fort blacksmith, he is a privileged character, but he doesn't act the part. He spreads the straw across the bottom of his bunk and lays out his bedroll. Off go the shoes, and he climbs up into the bunk to look at all the activity and to talk with his old friends.

"Brien, ya got your kids with you?"

"No, but I've got Jack Daniels," Brien answers as he plays with the fire in the fireplace.

"I've got Beanee-Weenees. Anybody want a can?"

"Yea, up here," and a can flies across the room.

"Y'all are a bunch of Boy Scouts," says one of the ladies.

"You're lucky we let girls in here," one of the younger reenactors retorts.

"Excuse me," Melinda, the site manager says as she walks in. "This is my fort, and you're lucky we let boys in." Everybody laughs at the kidding.

The noise never stops until you fall asleep.

"I've never been the last one awake," says Ralph, "so I don't know if it keeps going all night long."

Reenactors at a fort are a pretty tight bunch. Frequently, local reenactment units are the bulk of the garrison force of a fort. The monthly living-history program may be coordinated by them. They contribute a lot of their time, even when not reenacting, to the upkeep of the post. Volunteering their time for washing walls, cleaning the rafters, painting wood, and other restoration projects keeps an old fort intact.

Children participate in planned activities or make their own.

Rolling a hoop with a stick is a favorite pastime of garrison children.

GARRISON DUTY

There are preserved forts all over the United States that allow reenactors to come play soldiers. For the reenactor, this is the comfortable side of reenacting. Nearly all forts let the troops sleep in hay-stuffed bunks and have a big kitchen to make meals. The kitchen duties might be shared by the ladies of the fort, but all reenactors are responsible for cleaning their own dishes.

Since a battle is usually not a major focus at a fort, garrison reenactments emphasize the daily routine. Flag raising is done as a colors ceremony with all of the garrison falling in for dress parade. The soldiers fall in by company, and even the ladies make neat rows. The plan of the day is read and other announcements are made.

"Attention, battalion!" At the command, the drummer and fifer begin playing, and the flag goes fluttering up the flagpole.

"Remember, everyone be careful. Keep an eye on kids. Make sure sightseers stay off the edge of the walls, but be nice to them. We're here for them, they're not here for us.

"Mount, guard detail!"

To change the guard, the Sergeant of the Guard, with sash tied over his shoulder, assembles the guard detail to relieve the guard. A drummer and fifer accompany the guard detail to each post as they are formally replaced. Guard is posted at the sally port. More guards may walk the walls.

"Company commanders, take charge of your companies!"

Huge cannons stand as sentinels at Fort McHenry in Baltimore, Maryland, keeping enemy ships at bay.

One company remains on the parade ground for drill as a demonstration for the early visitors. The rest fall out to straighten up their quarters. Since the quarters are viewable by the public, they are usually kept very clean and orderly. With the soldiers standing by the bunks, an inspection is held. No anachronisms can be in sight, and reenactors care enough about the fort to sweep out the dust and cobwebs.

After the inspection, life in the bunkhouse includes singing, writing letters or reading the ever-present newspapers.

The companies rotate their drill several times a day, so there's something going on all the time. They practice facing movements, marching and musket firing. This serves to school the soldiers as well as to make an

impressive show for the public.

"Captain, we've caught us a deserter," one of the guard detail says as another escorts the prisoner at gunpoint.

"Very well, it seems we need a court-martial. Assemble the men."

The drummer and fifer call the men together, and the deserter is tried and found guilty. He is marched to a wall and shot by the firing squad. In a bit of comedy, the undertaker makes a skit out of his business.

There might be a mock skirmish, or a small battle, in the early afternoon, so about half of the men have to change coats, as the garrison is usually all Confederate or all Yankee. One side will hold the fort, the other attacks it.

Cannons at Fort Ward in Alexandria, Virginia, are positioned to protect the outskirts of Washington, D.C.

Looking down the barrel of a long-range cannon at Fort McHenry.

Looking out from the inside of a prison cell gives a dim picture of what it was like to be imprisoned at a fort.

NIGHT AT THE FORT

Tattoo is a dusk ceremony that some forts hold daily. It was originally a roll call to assemble the men before lights out. Tattoo can be very formal and should include field music. There may be a volley firing of rifles. Tattoo can be worked up to be a spectator event.

A candlelight tour of a fort can be magical. With the electric lights off, the 1860s image of a fort is enhanced by the flickering candles. Groups of tourists are brought around the fort to view card games, music playing, and other scenes of fort life.

"The latrine is where the soldiers do their necessaries," a lady explains to a group of tourists, as if she were conducting a regular fort tour.

She holds up her candle lantern and feigns a polite, "Oh my!" as she *accidentally* stumbles on a group of soldiers sitting in the fort's communal outhouse with their pants down. Nothing improper can be seen in the candlelight, and she moves the tourists quickly as if this scene hadn't been intended. Once the visitors move past the latrine, the soldiers can hardly contain their laughter.

At a tent set up in the corner of the parade ground, a woman and her children portray a family that has sought the protection of the fort. She rocks her baby to sleep while two girls sit by her side, staring into the campfire. No words are spoken at this tender vignette.

Moving on to another scene in the dim light, a soldier is crying (real tears) and telling the chaplain, "The Yankees are gonna move in tomorrow. I'm gonna die. I know it. I'm real scared."

"Let us pray, son." Both kneel and the chaplain continues, "Father, please grant your special blessings to this fort. Protect this lad and his comrades. But if it is your will that he should die in battle, end his suffering quickly and take him up in your arms to heaven."

The tour guide leads them into the Officers' Quarters. With the flames flickering from the hearth in the barracks, twenty men are singing a popular lament from the time of the war. There are candle lanterns on the walls, and the tour group is the quietest they have been since they entered the fort. The aroma of wood smoke adds to the atmosphere as the men's voices echo off the brick walls. Not a soldier's eye turns toward the group. They are not performing, yet they are at the peak of their performance. This is the inner sanctum of reenacting, and the tourists tiptoe out.

After the candlelight tour, a dance or ball is held and the fort becomes its most lively. Music from several places fills the air. It is easy to slip back in time and enjoy the festivities in comfortable surroundings. Lady reenactors particularly enjoy being able to dance and walk around the fort in their hoop dresses without worrying about getting dirty.

SUTLERS' ROW

Mat Murdock and his son, Anthony, have reenacted everywhere. Mat has worked on the staff of movies and supplied them their flags. Now he specializes in cloth, working with Elegant Finery, a company that sells specialized historical material to reenactors as well as to the theatrical community.

"I would call myself a stitch counter," Mat admits. That's someone who knows the exact weave a material ought to be. To Mat, it's not correct unless it's correct under the magnifying glass.

This weekend the Elegant Finery sutlery is set up at Fort Frederick in Maryland, right outside the fort as part of sutlers' row. A timeline event being held includes colonial to cowboy. Representing part of the Civil War contingent, Mat is in his U.S. Army officer's uniform. "I never go Confederate. I'm a Union man and that's what I believe. I'm as hardcore as the Georgia boys, only the other way."

During the day, Mat, Anthony and the rest of the staff have been selling cloth. None of them are in persona. They are the experts to whom reenactors from all periods come with their questions. They turn questions about clothing into sales.

"Let's close it down," and nobody objects. The tables outside the marquee are brought in. The side walls go up and the store is closed. There's still a bit of daylight left, and they open the forage boxes for food. Anthony shares his bologna and cheese sandwiches with the neighbors, and more people, including several other sutlers, gather around the table for snacks and beverages.

"Dad, I'm gonna go listen to some music," and Anthony gets up.

"I'll be over in a minute."

Around the campfire are people from all the eras, singing the favorites. There's a lot of Irish music, cowboy songs and the inevitable sea chanteys. The great thing about a timeline

Sutlers' row, with its wide aisles, is a great place to shop or visit.

A Lincoln impersonator lies in state for hours at a time at this timeline event at Rosehill Cemetery in Chicago, Illinois.

event is this blend of characters and culture. There are knee breeches and shell jackets, Quakers and Redcoats, even a few kilts.

PERMANENT GARRISON

Because most forts are visited daily by tourists, they are a high-profile form of living history. There are a few forts that pay a core staff of reenactors and allow them to live at the fort site. In Michigan, Fort Mackinac has a summer staff that interprets history to thousands of visitors. Blacksmithing, woodworking and music are regularly demonstrated.

Ken Chambers retired from his job in Saginaw, Michigan, giving him more time for reenacting. He's done all the Michigan events and has made long trips to places such as Fort Zachary Taylor, Florida; Gettysburg, Pennsylvania; and Franklin, Tennessee. He hops

periods and has reenacted voyageur and East Coast colonial. To top it all off, he is a U.S. Navy veteran. A reenactor has a little extra stature if he has been in the real military.

He lives in Midland, Michigan, but he's rarely there. Up on Mackinac Island, he is part of the permanent garrison. "I love it. They give me a place to sleep, and every morning I put my uniform on. I portray a sergeant who was actually stationed at the fort for years. I know as much about him as anyone can, and I've visited his grave site.

"I carry out the daily duties and give tours to the visitors. My favorite thing is to play music. I can do a little melody on almost every type of popular instrument of the 1800s. Sometimes I sit on a bench and play the concertina, or I join the others in a bit of singing. That's when I feel like I'm most portraying life at the fort."

A trooper salutes his dead president at a reenactment of Lincoln's viewing in Chicago.

Women's Reenactment Activities

Almost as many women are involved in reenacting as men, and their activities are broad and varied

Some families accompany their husbands to the field, attending to the household chores around camp. The tents are their new homes. Families are the lifeblood of many reenactment units.

The hostesses, with their friendly smiles, are the center of the company. They're the ones who stay around the campfire, making sure the unit functions as a team. They know everybody's name and make everyone feel at home.

The only time families are forced out of camp is when it is part of a battle scenario. When the time comes, they run, like they're being chased out. Refugee rushes to safety have been subplots of battle reenactments. All of the civilians can participate. The women and children are forced to find refuge with nearby military units when their homes

Waiting in camp while your loved one is away can be a lonely experience.

Afternoon teas give the women a chance to socialize and display their reproduction clothing.

become threatened. As property is burned and the countryside laid waste, civilian women and children seek the army's protection and stay as near to the military as possible.

Several reenactments have included scenarios that actively involve refugees, including their mass movement with the army. Women, with their children, represent the destitute condition of these people on the move.

Some women are drawn to reenacting by the ladies' teas and dance. They may have first gotten involved in reenacting with husbands or brothers and at that time wore camp dresses. Then after research, they buy patterns and fabrics to make fancier dresses. Many ladies dress quite elegantly and some like to display their bead and jewelry collections. China, silver and furniture become the play toys of those who can afford it.

Whatever the activity, there is a kinship

The older girls do the heavy washing in a nearby stream.

The little girls wash shirts for 25 cents to help keep the men's clothes clean.

Families such as these two go to reenactments to take care of the troops by feeding them and caring for their needs.

with ancestors, a spirituality in what the women do. Many women have an especially strong sense of having lived in the past.

"My current lifetime is only one of many," explains one teenage girl. "Some lives are male, some are female. They are experienced by my soul that travels from one body in time to another. The actual mechanism perplexes me, but there is a definite order and purpose to being born again.

"I believe part of the duty of one's existence is to reach back and feel what awareness came before this present lifetime," she continues. "There is a window that opens up to my prior lives, and I can feel it. Time pulls like a vacuum cleaner. It's continuous. Once the link is started, it becomes a two-way street. There is a two-way feeling of energy that draws me."

This young girl was drafted by her father, the commander, to fill in the ranks of a Confederate battle in Clinton, Georgia.

A cavalrywoman rides into camp with her hair tucked up, but it glistens in the sun and gives away her secret.

FIGHTING LADIES

A surprising number of females enjoy portraying those women who passed themselves off as male soldiers. Civil War women who felt the call to arms had to disguise themselves. They passed through a sloppy entrance examination and made trips to the privies by themselves. Since many young boys were in the service, sometimes not even the voice gave away the woman's secret.

"I can be a convincing soldier as long as I don't talk," says one reenactor. "Being a soldier is really a way of walking, of how you hold your head and shoulders. When I do that right, I'm a success."

"I have researched one of my Civil War ancestors," another woman explains. "It all started when I fell heir to my great-great-grandfather's diary. I read of his camping in the winter in Virginia and of all the false starts. I don't think historians today appreciate the difficulties of moving an army. I didn't until I read about it in the diary. So now I'm out here, honoring his memory."

Another lady soldier clarifies her feelings,

"I tune in to the warrior spirit. I know I have gone through many lifetimes. I can remember—or I've got some pretty good guesses—on what some of them were. I was a soldier during the time of the Civil War, I can feel it. Reenacting helps find the way into my past. It makes me remember details."

"Women can be more sensitive to the inner workings of time and reincarnation," a cavalry trooperette explains. "For me, it's like dreaming. It usually happens after I've reenacted two or three reenactments in a row. I begin to receive an insight into the war.

"Late Saturday night in my tent, as I drift

After the battle is over, this soldier cleans her gun barrel with water.

Above: Holding her rifle and blending in with her platoon, a female trooper is proud to be following her flag.

off to sleep, some dreams are more than real. I feel the fear of being at battle, the sheer terror of it all," she says. "Playing down the side of the rocks are the trees that have seen the gathering of forces. There is a huddling of spirits. Out they charge, and I see the enemy coming at us. I find myself wondering if I'll survive this fight. Sometimes I awake truly frightened. It's a very intense feeling, and I feel it contains my experience from a previous existence."

Nancy has achieved the look she was striving for to play the role of Ned.

Demonstrating how a woman can pass as a man at a reenactment, a lady Yankee soldier explains to a group of schoolchildren, "Loose-fitting clothing was the popular style in the mid-1800s, so the baggy pants can easily disguise a female form. I pack my hair up in my forage cap and keep my neck well shaved, so even close up, it looks like I have short hair."

Another lady explains, "My uniform is like that of Vivandieres serving with a French Louisiana unit. Like the battle tactics themselves, many things were modeled from Napoleon Bonaparte's army. Over the pants is this short, heavy skirt. The coat is a separate piece, covering the blouse with a sewn-in vest line and a lot of buttons.

"I go to the battles with the men, marching in line, but I don't carry a gun. Instead, I carry an extra large bottle of water to help out the company."

And so it is that many women play the role of soldier, each with her own character and identity with the past.

MEDICAL IMPRESSIONS FOR THE LADY REENACTOR

Since the earliest days of fighting, women have dressed the wounds of warriors, but in the 1860s they were desperately needed.

"I came to this camp as an individual and found plenty of work. In the hospital tent, I do what I can to help the medical needs of the army and the bloodstained soldiers," explains a young nurse. "I hear there's going to be a battle. There'll be a lot with murderous wounds. We'll do what we can for them."

Reenactors who are wives and mothers often work medical impressions at the battle. "I'm not a doctor, but I've been doing what I can," says one mom. "Even without their deadly wounds, they need a lot of water run to them. On hot days, we carry ice out in canvas buckets."

"Almost every building around here has become a hospital. They laid them out all over the floor, until there's just no more room. We use our books for pillows, and our carpets

In a field hospital, ladies volunteer to care for the troops as they come in wounded.

absorb their blood." The men on those books and carpets are really resting reenactors, glad for the break after the battle. They do a good job of portraying grievously wounded soldiers, while getting a bit of a nap and some tender care.

A period nun gives comfort and advice to a few men on a short break.

LADIES AUXILIARIES

Women in camp have the option of representing the hometown efforts at the time of the war. There are several versions of aid societies and Sanitary Commissions, who campaigned for improving the quality of living standards for the soldiers.

Ladies' auxiliaries can be local in nature, representing women organized to help particular reenactment units. The aid society can be organized to help a particular reenactment, such as the Soldier's Aid Society in Selma, Alabama. They represent women who would sew or make clothing, but they are also the behind-the-scenes help with the battle at Selma.

Ladies from home welcome the troops from battle with the display of their precious flag.

WAIT FOR THE WAGON

Will you come with me, my Phyllis dear,
To yon Blue Mountain free,
Where blossoms smell the sweetest,
Come rove along with me;
It's every Sunday morning,
When I am by your side,
We'll jump into the wagon
And all take a ride.
CHORUS (repeat after each verse):
Wait for the wagon, wait for the wagon,
Wait for the wagon and we'll all take
     a ride.

Where the river runs like silver
And the birds they sing so sweet,
I have a cabin, Phyllis dear,
And something good to eat;
Come listen to my story,
It will relieve my heart;
So jump into the wagon,
And off we will start.

Do you believe, my Phyllis dear,
Old Mike, with all his wealth,

Can make you half so happy
As I, with youth and health?
We'll have a little farm,
A horse, a pig and cow;
And you will mind the dairy,
While I do guide the plow.

Your lips are red as poppies,
Your hair so slick and neat,
All braided up with dahlias,
And hollyhocks so sweet.
It's every Sunday morning,
When I am by your side,
We'll jump into the wagon,
And all take a ride.

Together on life's journey,
We'll travel till we stop,
And if we have no trouble,
We'll reach the happy top;
Then come with me, sweet Phyllis dear,
My dear, my lovely bride,
We'll jump into the wagon
And all take a ride.

In a calm part of a Confederate camp, a Soldier's Aid Society member explains, "They ought to call it the bandage society, we cut and roll so many of them, Even without the pressing need of battle, we make bandages to make sure our boys have enough."

Many women are great cooks. When food is cooked in camp, it is well shared. Sometimes a small charge subsidizes a good cause or defrays the expense of someone else's reenacting. Cookies, cakes, jerkies and sausages are favorites with the soldiers. Food wares are provided on an underground mom-and-pop vending system.

"We have a line of peas that stretches, by railroad, from here to Illinois," serves up a lady passing out food to the waiting reenactors. This Saturday night meal is courtesy of the local historical society. The reenactors have focused attention on a lot of local history. This benefits a town, and the ladies' auxiliary, known as the Sanitary Commission, holds the reenactment barbecue and get-together to show appreciation.

"I can't believe you have this many cookies left over," I said in astonishment.

"No, take the whole bucket. That bucket held the flour from which I baked all the cookies. We sold them a quarter apiece. That's just a small portion of what we sold. We want to

Many women bear the traditional roles of food preparation. As hostesses, they try to make everyone feel comfortable.

earn enough for a bigger tent. There'll be more room for people to sit down. Maybe, by next year."

THE OLDEST PROFESSION

"Come, get your picture taken with me, soldier!" extols the young woman dressed in a muslin camisole and pantaloons.

Several other girls stroll out, just as scantily clad. The boy gladly gives up five dollars to get his picture taken with these beauties. This tent in West Virginia is a favorite with reenactors and spectators alike.

At a Civil War Round Table seminar, a lecturer dramatizing a lady of the evening discloses, "When there are large gatherings of men, there is money to be made by supplying them with the comforts of women. Generally the evidence of the prevalence of prostitutes in the war is skimpy or deliberately destroyed. Letters that spoke of the pleasures of the flesh were not often saved by relatives. Sin was kept a secret. But we know there were many women who catered to the physical pleasures of the army."

Some reenactors who portray ladies of ill-repute do so as a parody. Walking around in period underwear, they are a portable comedy theater. "You know how we got our name?" one tart asks. "We hung around General *Hooker's* camps."

"They've got on more than these tourists, but we hoot and howl," a soldier says. "We know it would be scandalous to walk around like that in the 1860s."

It's all part of the fun.

Reenacting the oldest profession in pretty underpinnings is one way to stay cool.

81

Groups such as this one enjoy
singing and playing period
music for reenactors as well
as tourists.

The Social Graces

As with most events planned for large crowds, the social activities are a tremendous draw and help give Civil War reenacting its character. Day and night, there are scheduled frolics and more casual affairs that allow reenactors and spectators alike to interact as if they were back in the 1860s.

All throughout the camps, soldiers play and sing period songs that help set the scene and transport the mind to a time long past. Folk stylists play such instruments as accordion, concertina, harmonica, guitar, fiddle, tin whistle and minstrel banjo. There is a litany of songs that are known by all of the seasoned reenactors. They sing this music marching into battle or late at night around the campfire.

Groups of musicians also perform in more formal concert settings, replicating period music and instrumental styles. Regimental bands fall into this category. Because a band marching at the front of a regiment can better be heard if the instruments point toward the

These ladies enjoy their
time together and traveling
to a previous era.

people marching behind, the brass instruments are designed to be played while resting on the players' shoulders, with the bells of the horns angled toward the rear.

Fife and drum corps give concerts and also march into battle with the regiments. Martial airs are an inspiration to the troops. They serve much the same military function as the brass bands, but often draw their players from individual companies as did their historical counterparts.

SHOPPING SUTLERS' ROW

Most of the things reenactors need are available from sutlers, whose tents create rows of casual browsing and serious shopping for the reenactor looking for provisions. From raw leather and cloth to finely made ball gowns, almost everything you can imagine from the 1860s can be found at these Civil War shopping malls.

During the war, sutlers would set up elaborate marquee tents for longer encampments. Some were photographic studios; some sold fresher food than the army could obtain. A dapper soldier might find a hat to his liking. Writing materials for keeping in touch with the folks at home were essential. Newspapers were in high demand as were tobacco and liquor. A sutler was not supposed to sell liquor to private soldiers, which meant the sutler could demand a higher price for this illegal item.

Modern sutlers concentrate on clothing and leather goods more than their old-time counterparts. Besides uniform items, bumper stickers, flags and T-shirts are for sale at all reenactments, though such items are often considered contraband at a strict reenactment and have to be sold under the table.

Rarely would ladies' items have been sold at an 1860s sutlery. But at a reenactment, they are popular. Not everyone has time to make their own ball gown nor the skills to turn raw leather into footwear. And what a delight to find a string of old glass beads that complement an outfit.

Once a reenactor is outfitted, he or she is suited to attend the social gatherings that take place day and night.

Sutler businesses are often run by couples who enjoy a roving lifestyle and meeting thousands of people who share their interest in history.

Some sutlers cater to just the ladies.

LADIES' TEA

Ladies' tea is more a mood than an event. On the surface, it's a traveling dress-craft display with a chance to show off dresses in the critical light of day. There might be a lecture on period attire or mannerisms.

Underneath the surface is a feeling of transcendence. "We are all sitting here in another time," a lady whispers to her neighbor.

Sitting beneath the shade of a pleasant springtime garden are the ladies attending the event at Selma. They are enjoying lunch on the ground, listening to classical guitar strains, lightly played. The soft warmth of the sun dapples down between the shadows of the leaves. The historic house is open for tours and is a beehive of activity.

Yet, on the lawns, there is a feeling of sadness and nostalgia that this style of living has long gone. There are a hundred gentlewomen there, but it's relatively quiet as many prefer to ponder the moment.

An afternoon tea becomes an educational opportunity to learn what to wear, how to sew, and tips for being a lady of the 1860s.

Touring old plantation homes is a treat the ladies sometimes get to enjoy in the afternoons.

This young couple is
ready to attend the
Saturday-night ball.

OFFICERS' RECEPTIONS

An Officers' Reception is limited to one
side or the other. For example, there might be
a United States Army Officers' Reception,
where the commander and his staff host a
party for the Union officers and their wives.
Naturally, this would be at the commander's
tent in Federal camp.

There is an air of exclusivity, and this military gathering can be stuffy, but that is a part of
the attraction of the Officers' Reception.
Typical background music for this social would
be a banjo picker or classical-guitar player.

"Colonel, it's good to see you again. I trust
your men got their share of mischief today,"
the Federal commander says.

"Yes, sir, they did. The gave the rebels a
good fight and ran them off the hill."

"Well, bully," is the period-correct reply.

Getting ready for the ball when in the field means washing up anywhere you can.

THE BALL

The ball or camp dance is so essential to reenacting that few reenactments fail to hire musicians for the dance. Reenactors come to the ball in Confederate, Union or civilian attire and all mix together. For many ladies, their favorite part of the reenactment is the ball.

"Sing 'Southern Girl'," requests a lady waiting in line for the bus that will transport her to the hall where the ball will be held tonight.

"I'd be glad to, ma'am," and the strains of the harmonica play over gut-strung guitar arpeggios. The melody gives way to the words. The ball is a big event and transportation can get backed up. So, musicians are hired to sing for those waiting at the bus stop.

At the other end of the bus ride, Billie Joe Sawyers is playing chords on the concertina, the melody on his braced harmonica, and his

The women help each other with final touches before putting on their ball gowns.

feet are beating out the rhythm on the tambourines. Billie is a smiling "one-man band."

It is already crowded in the hall, and the band is about to start. Once inside, there is magic, with one of the finest string bands calling the dances. Colonel Rambo gets up on the stage and says, "We're going to have enough Grand Marches to include everybody, even if we have to do it four or five times.

"Let's make the first row right in the center, couples two by two. All right, are we ready?"

And a big "whooooooooo" yell builds across the room.

The upright bass starts in at a walking pace for this warm-up instrumental promenade, and the rest of the 97th Regimental String Band bring flowery perfection to the period music with guitar and fiddle.

The couples come back four-abreast, then eight-abreast, then sixteen-abreast, then somehow thirty-two people squeeze in shoulder-to-shoulder for the review. They keep doing this until everyone gets a chance to be a part of the Grand March.

At a different ball in Kentucky, but with the same spirit, "It's Virginia reel time. Gather in groups of seven couples for the Virginia reel. Squeeze it in. Step lively, or you'll miss out."

"Bow to your partners!" and each of the group steps forward to bow in line, a part of this formal dance that everyone loves to do.

"Right hand round!" Clasping right hands, couples twirl then do it again with:

"Left hand round!"

"Both hands round!"

"Doe-see-doe!" with their hands behind their backs.

"Lead couple, show 'em how it's done and sashay down!"

"Promenade down the street, with everyone that you meet!" and everyone takes a twirl with the lead couple.

**A high-spirited Virginia
Reel is the highlight of
every reenactment
dance.**

Reenactors lead a Grand
March while the band
plays.

"Promenade back and lead 'em around!"

"Make a bridge, make 'em all go under!" and, a couple at a time, the dance line squeezes together under the bridge made by the arms of the lead couple.

"Go back home and do it again!"

In a camp at Port Hudson, Louisiana, another guitarist tells the audience, "They say I'm too old to fight in the line of battle. I'm telling you I'm here today to urge you on in the good steps. Let's try a Tennessee Two-Step." And then there is a lot more dancing.

The dancing was light and lively, the company was grand, but when it is over, it was too short.

"So that, ladies and gentlemen, is our good-night song of the evening." The splendor is over, and a hundred hearts are sad.

The ladies are exquisite and the men are dashing in their period formal wear.

A minister strives to nourish souls by preaching the gospel at a Sunday service.

PREACHING THE GOSPEL

When times are hard, people turn to God. The battlefield is a fruitful mission field for the preacher, and many reenactors feel God's call to preach and minister at reenactments.

A religious service of one type or another is held at almost every reenactment. Some are re-creations of services held during the war. For instance, an ordained priest might deliver the sacraments in Latin, the way it would have been done in the 1860s.

A Southern reenacting pastor might warn his flock, "You could die in battle today, and your first thought must be of preparing your souls for heaven. Are you right with God?" he eulogizes.

Playing the part of an abolitionist minister, a reenactor urges the Union troops, "Carry

Singing to lighten the heart is a common practice at Sunday-morning prayer meetings.

out God's plan for wiping away slavery from the South. Reunite this Union and make it free for all mankind," he beseeches with radical fervor. "I see a new birth of freedom, under God, that will come from the slaves being freed."

There are also evangelists who care for the twentieth-century souls of the reenactors. Some are on fire and preach in a traditional, passionate manner. The altar call leaves the realm of

reenactment and becomes real as people accept their Savior at the religious service.

Witnessing can occur as the preachers talk to individuals about their religious beliefs. "If a soldier takes a hit in battle and falls," Roger tells his congregation, "I'm going to give him this wartime tract and tell him a little bit about Jesus. I'll pray with him just as any army chaplain would pray with the wounded and dying. For me and for many I pray with, the prayers are real."

Once again, the line is blurred. Is this now, or is it then? It's hard to tell, but every year, hundreds of thousands seek out the experiences of spirit that come with being a time traveler. Civil War reenacting—it's so real, you think you are there.